1001 Decorating Ideas
Bedrooms

Galahad Books • New York City

Contents

Introduction

The bedroom is the most personal room in the house and should reflect the personalities and needs of its occupants. The master bedroom should be an oasis, a place to relax or have a cup of tea away from the bustle of the rest of the house. Children's rooms should be fun places that can be used as play areas, studies, and personal retreats. The guest room should be a comfortable rest area for visitors, with well-planned closet and storage space; but it should also serve the family's needs when there are no guests—perhaps double as a den, sewing room, or office.

All bedrooms should be designed for comfort and convenience. The beds should be comfortable, lights positioned so that you can read in bed without strain, rugs placed so that you can touch something soft when getting out of bed, curtains or shades hung to control daylight. But in addition, they should all be designed to please your personal tastes, to provide a restful and very private environment.

The bedrooms on the following pages should give you some decorating ideas for your own master bedroom, childrens' rooms, and guest rooms.

Many thanks are given to 1,001 Decorating Ideas.

Chapter 1
Master Bedrooms

Your master bedroom should be extremely comfortable and warmly welcoming. And it should be designed to suit your personal needs — it might have a corner where you can needlepoint quietly under a window, an entertainment unit with a television and stereo, or an area that you can use as an office or study.

The modular storage wall used here has migrated from the living room and been transformed into a handsome, queen-sized headboard. Sliding tufted vinyl sections hide storage space and also provide a backrest for reading in bed. A "bridge" with built-in spotlights stretches over the headboard and two flanking pier cabinets. The bed and windows are covered with patterned sheets.

Photo: Everette Short/Design: Evan Frances, ASID, and J. Christopher Jones

This bedroom is a primer lesson in how to decorate with "the naturals." Bedspread, pillows, and draperies in neutral tones and nubby textures complement the cane and oak grain wood furniture. The brown earth tone of the carpeting, the taupe and bisque hues of the painted walls, and the nature studies on the walls complete the country look. Vertically mounted track lights provide illumination for the statues, as well as nocturnal reading light.

8

Here is a practical closet for a master bedroom. It has double-louvered wood doors and vinyl-coated, ventilated wire shelves that provide maximum storage efficiency. They won't split, crack, warp, or mildew — the spaces between the wires guarantee free circulation of air.

Photos: Keith Scott Morton/Design: Scruggs-Myers & Assoc.

Design: Carleton Varney

A mélange of furniture styles is unified with a single floral print. For private chats or tea for two, the room is furnished with a pair of tub chairs around a tiny table. Simple draperies are used to frame, but not conflict with, the glorious view of the gardens.

This high-ceilinged and spacious room has a gray and wine color scheme, splashed with teal and yellow. There's a breakfast table in the corner, a sewing machine, and a comfortable reading chair.

The soft blue- and green-striped towels in the sauna pick up the bedroom color scheme.

This master bedroom suite is comprised of a spacious bedroom, sauna, bathroom, and exercise room. A cane-and-wood room divider with a Mondrian-like geometric design separates the sleeping area from the seating area in the long room. A dressing and clothing storage area is concealed behind it as well. The mirror, seen upon entering, creates depth and is exactly duplicated on the other side of the divider. A glass-shelved étagère defines the sleeping area while artfully displaying potted plants and sculpture. Three rattan panels that slide to the side to reveal the window form an elegant headboard. Set against a sand-colored carpet, the platform bed appears to float above the floor. Modular seating units in the entertainment and relaxation area at the other end of the room are upholstered in the same fabric as the bedspread. This adult retreat is a well-balanced combination of sleek design and primitive accessories in a serene beige, blue, and green setting.

Photography: Bill Hedrich/Design: Patricia Laughman and J. Christopher Jones

11

Photo: Marianne Engberg/Design: Jerry Hanover, Joe Minicucci

This French-inspired room has a Louis XV canopy bed and screens. The floor is covered with white octagonal tile with pink insets. Custom-made mirrored doors, set between the columns, expand the room's size.

This elegant room is furnished with cherry-finished, Colonial-style pieces. Three different fabrics are used for the walls, window, table, chair, and bed coverings.

Photos: Vince Lisanti

Do you collect, cherish, and decorate with mementos? Then let your bedroom be a tribute to tradition, with lots of lovely old-fashioned touches. The most charming is the double-knot fringe trim on the bedspread, pillow shams, table skirt, and draperies. Add a milk-glass oil lamp, porcelain wash bowl, and a pair of primitive portraits — all are perfectly at home in this easy-care bedroom that's prim enough in spirit to elicit approval from a Victorian.

Photo: Vince Lisanti

Subtle hues — gray, blue, and pale yellow — counterpoint bold patterns in this master bedroom. Wallpaper is used with coordinating fabric on the bedspread. The border has a lattice design, which extends onto the custom canopy. To solidify the color scheme and provide a surface to rest the eye, the floor is carpeted in an unpatterned gray-blue. Mini-blinds, behind light blue textured sheer curtains, provide privacy and light control.

Photo: Darwin Davidson/Design: Peg Walker

This room has been embellished in "brass" and "chrome" with carefully applied self-adhesive. The once-white platform bed is now sparkling chrome. Brass cutouts on the lamps and narrow bands of chrome on the lamp shades echo the glitter. Behind the bed, decoupage flowers add even more sparkle.

Paneling and beams give a country character to this bedroom. Thin blinds on the window and patio door control light and air. Windows are left undraped, giving an open feeling. A floral fabric covers the bed and chair. And a shirred-on-the-rod valance and draperies of the same garden-look fabric create a romantic demi-canopy behind the bed. The desk beneath the window serves as a convenient night table.

Photos: Vince Lisanti/Design: Arthur Burke

Photo: Everette Short/Design: Ellyn Carol Hirsch

This master suite is a study in sugar and spice. For sweetness and serenity, a quiet, neutral color scheme and a romantic swagged sheer curtain are used. The graphic design along the side wall adds a dash of spice.

The Louis XV *bérgères* in this lovely provincial bedroom are covered in two fabrics. The white carpet contrasts sharply with the country colors of the wall covering and the five coordinating fabrics.

A bedroom wall gets the full window treatment — soft-fold valances flanked by burlap curtains edged in matching stripes.

Photo: Idaka/Design: Evan Frances, ASID/Interior architecture: Claire Golan

▼   Two different window treatments in the
same room complement each other by the use
of matching fabric. An elegant balloon shade that
billows over a window and long, ruffled, shirred
curtains on the balcony doors are perfect addi-
tions to this romantic setting.

Bedroom, study, and entertaining areas are incorporated into this large room. The modular storage units, all 30 inches wide, include a drop-front desk with a lighted interior and an open unit with a pull-out shelf to hold a television and stereo. The bed has inset lights over it and a storage head-board with removable pillows.

Photos: Idaka/Design: Evan Frances, ASID, and Claire Golan, ASID

Photo: Alan Hicks/Design: Russell English & Mark Perry

Bits of the countryside are displayed in this Gay 90's-style room. The angels were gathered from old churches and buildings, and the rest of the furniture was found in barns, shops, and at auctions. The two corner windows are treated as one window, with a cornice and softly draped hangings.

This sophisticated retreat pares down furnishings to the barest essentials — a built-in shelf for a headboard holds a reading lamp and serves as a handy backrest to prop up piles of pillows. For color, four medium pastels — seafoam green, chamois, periwinkle blue, and dusty rose — are linked, surprisingly, by black and white. For pattern, there's a four-way play: blossoming poppies, multi-colored stripes, mono-stripes, and a basket weave.

Photo: Everette Short/Design: Evan Frances, ASID

This blue and yellow room has a combination of brick and flowered-wallpaper walls (below). The bedspread and table cover have a fabric border, which is repeated in the shutters (above).

Photo: Yuichi Idaka/Design: Richard Honquest and J. Christopher Jones

Because the size of this master bedroom is extraordinarily generous, it can handle large-scale, traditionally styled furniture — including a magnificent broken-pediment highboy and a big floral print in the draperies, bedspread, and dust ruffle. A rocking chair and an excellent floor lamp sit in a reading corner with a view of tree tops. An Oriental motif, a compatible mix with traditional furnishings, is introduced via graphics and a red lacquer box.

With weathered wood overhead and soft-green carpet underfoot, the master bedroom is a relaxing mix of mellow tones and naturals. Modular pier storage cabinets, connected by a lighted bridge, frame a mirror.

Photo: Everette Short/Design: John Mascheroni and J. Christopher Jones

Lots of colorful accessories stand out against the "white shell" created by the bright white walls, white ceiling, and white rug.

Design: Peg Walker, ASID

This Louis XV, provincial-style dresser is used to create a room with an 18th-century French atmosphere. On the walls, windows, and window seat is a beautiful toile-de-Jouy in the traditional red-on-white colors.

Photo: Alderman Studio/Design: Jo Howlett, ASID

Situated away from children, guests, and noise, this master suite is both quiet and elegant. Gray walls blend with the gentle mauve-pink carpeting. A boldly quilted bed cover and draperies contrast with the delicate bamboo bench and chairs. The Oriental motif is evident in the shape of the headboard and cornice, the egret painting over the bed, and the rich raspberry ginger jar lamps.

Photo: Floyd Jillson/Design: June Gussin

This modern bedroom is sleek and flexible, with streamlined storage units instead of traditional space-consuming bedroom furniture. The white furniture shown here includes drawers, cabinets, adjustable shelves, slide-out trays, and a drop-lid desk with interior lighting. The upholstered storage headboard behind the platform bed is great for reading or TV viewing — and it can house extra blankets or linens. The wall arrangement shown turns a corner, providing maximum utility in minimum space. Wall lamps above the headboard swing out for convenient lighting.

Photos: Everette Short/Design: Evan Frances, ASID

Photo: Dennis Purse/Design: Jim de Martin

An Early American mood is created with boldly colorful elements. The washable wall covering is reproduced from an original Jacobean fabric imported from England in the 17th century by an American merchant. Its "turkey red" and antique greens provide a colorful background for a kingly bed with wooden tester, headboard carved with linen-fold panels, and rope-turned posts. Heavy fringe on window- and bed-hangings adds an important textural contrast.

This sumptuous master bedroom is two rooms made into one. Grass-green carpet brings the outdoors in and is a wonderfully neutral background for the yellow textured wall covering and the colorful chintz.

Photos: Vince Lisanti/Design: Nance Randol Interiors

Photo: Hedrich-Blessing/Design: Montgomery Ward Home Furnishings Staff

Romantically tented and curtained, a crewel-covered, queen-sized bed dominates the minute bedchamber of this master suite. Balloon shades soften two small windows, yet conserve vital space. Perfect for reading in bed, twin pin-up lamps are floor space savers, too. The bed is flanked by small-scale furnishings — a pedestal table and a semainier.

◄   Warmed by a free-standing fireplace, the master suite's sitting room holds crewel-upholstered chaises. The "tent flap" window treatment is one piece of lined and quilted fabric hung from a wood frame. Split three-quarters up from the bottom, the curtain is tied back to allow light to enter.

▼   Traditional bedroom furnishings require more room than a modular wall, but if you have the space, they're always appealing. Here is a restful retreat bathed in golden tones. The luxurious four-poster bed is bedecked with quilted bedspread, dust ruffle, and lacy crocheted afghan. The bed, footstool, "Bachelor Chest" with burl front, night stand, and "Lady's Desk" with wing chair are mahogany solids and veneers.

Photo: Alderman Studio

35

Design: Nance Randol

This bedroom is a marvelous mixture of the modern and the antique — of the priceless and the least-priced furnishings. A Victorian chair, a framed fan, a marble-topped chest, and Tiffany accessories are heirlooms. The painted desk, on the other hand, is a secondhand find. And the trim used for drapery tiebacks, toss pillows and picture frames is an inexpensive touch. Print fabric is fashioned into a bedspread and slipcovers for the chaise and headboard. An antique magazine rack (under window) was converted to a yarn holder.

For the forever romantic, here is an appealing storybook bedroom. The Persian-design carpet sounds the sole strong note of pattern. As a backdrop for the room, one color serenely sets the scene — here, it's deep blue-green but any other subtle shade woven into the carpet would serve as elegantly. Deep blue-green covers the walls, softens the ceiling, and is painted onto the wide board floor. Everything else is white: White sheer curtains caught up with ruffled tiebacks and skirted with a matching café curtain; white quilted, fitted one-piece bedspread with a mock dust ruffle of shirred eyelet embroidery and matching pillow shams; white gossamer canopy cover. To complete the white theme: a pristine snowscape above the bed, white-shaded lamp beside it, and a white wicker table.

Chapter 2
Girls' Rooms

When designing a child's room, the expression of personality is paramount — age or sex shouldn't matter if the room reflects your child's individuality. A girl's bedroom should not only be a sleeping area, but a recreational and educational space as well.

Traditional bedrooms bathed in pretty provincial patterns invite lingering during wake-up hours. Here, a playful mini-floral print turns a dreary attic into a flower bower. The window seat, with matching fabric-covered pad and pillows, provides a cozy spot for reading or needlework — with storage beneath.

Photo: Photographic House/Design: Dorothy Wyeth Dobbins

Design: Carleton Varney

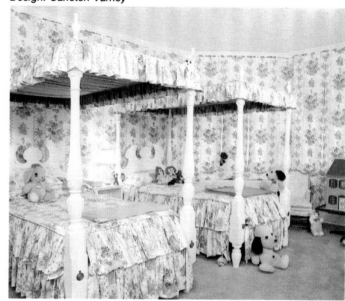

The odd shape of this little girl's room is camouflaged by using a single print everywhere. The puffy shades were used because of a protruding radiator.

A deliciously feminine room is established here with the eyelit-trimmed canopy and draperies. The headboard wall is covered in white paneling, which coordinates with the furniture. Color contrast is provided by the red in the international doll collection, as well as by the silk flowers. Carpeting in light avocado tones covers the floor. Track lights provide grow light for plants as well as illumination for the closet. Special hooks attached to the track permit hanging plants in front of the windows.

Photos: Everette Short/Design: Evan Frances, ASID, and J. Christopher Jones

Vertically mounted track lighting saves floor and desk-top space in this small room and offers flexible lighting. The top sphere is angled for general room light; the center sphere spotlights toys on the window ledge; and the bottom sphere provides perfect light for desk work. ▼

▼ In this room, paneling is applied to the top of the walls, fabric to the bottom. Matching fabric is used for the bedspread and tent canopy, and to cover the closet doors.

Photo: Vince Lisanti/Design: Arthur Burke, ASID

41

Butterflies and lots of color compensate for few furnishings in this room. The furniture is painted to conceal its modest origins. The Parsons table was bought unfinished; the blue-and-white-painted dresser and the nightstand were garnered at a garage sale.

Wake up in a bower of flowers in this romantic bedroom. A floral print, as delicately traced as fine porcelain, patterns walls and pillows, skirts the bed, covers the table. The single print lavished all over helps unify the room's awkward jogs.

A bright floral print fabric used for the walls, bedspreads, and flouncy shirred curtains adds excitement to a room devoid of architectural interest.

To give this room its look, fabric is stapled onto the mirror frame, screen, desk, headboard, latticework sliding window screens, and the acoustical tile on the wall behind the bed. The platform bed is a wonderful world unto itself, with built-in audio equipment and storage in the headboard, and a spot for snacking at the foot.

Photo: Ernest Silva Studio/Design: Carl Fuchs

This young lady's bedroom gathers furniture from different centuries to create a room with a "period" ambience. The butterfly table, serving as a nightstand, was originally a 1725 New England specialty based on Jacobean design. The rocker, indigenous to America, was created in 1745 by adding a curved support to a Windsor chair. The Chippendale-style chest and low four-poster bed are late 18th-century style. These period pieces combine beautifully with the contemporary brass lamp and the 20th-century carpet.

Photo: Rick Smith, Norling Studios/Design: Martha Ward, ASID

This romantic dream of a room has a storybook bed with an all-white comforter, eyelet-edged pillows, and crystal-pleated dust ruffle.

Photo: Kal Weyner/Design: Marjorie Axthelm Scholly

irls too dream of becoming pilots and flying high in the sky, so in this girl's room floats a fanciful hot-air balloon, a spritely butterfly, and a biplane — all waft gently in the upper air currents. Butter-yellow walls and yellow pine flooring are a sunny background for the white finished furnishings with yellow accent striping. A modular storage wall of pier cabinets containing chests and a desk with chair, and joined by a light bridge, is sweetened with a posy painting and serpentine shaping.

Photo: Everette Short/Design: John Mascheroni and J. Christopher Jones

This bedroom fit for a belle only looks fragile. Actually, the dainty, lace-edged polyester/rayon print is machine washable.

Photo: Hans Van Nes /Design: Shirley Regendahl

to: Yuichi Idaka/Design: Richard Honquest and J. Christopher Jones

In this little girl's bedroom, toys, dolls, and a Snoopy telephone provide playmates. A bright yellow bird-and-flower chintz adorns her canopy, bedspread, shams, all walls, and the ruffled drapery hung from a fabric-covered rod. The handsome cherry four-poster bed and dresser will serve from little girl to teenage years, and then go on to accommodate guests after she leaves home.

47

◄ **S**ome children are charmed by country-cottage interiors. The little girl who lives here likes her room pastel-pretty and populated by plenty of small creatures, some of whom are having tea. Patchwork patterns in pastel shades form the backdrop for lemon-yellow furniture. Patchwork wall covering wraps up and over the walls and window shades, covers door panels, and refurbishes a run-down Parsons table.

Design: Susan Sackner and Sylvia Schloss

◄ Not many young romantics can resist a canopy. Unfortunately, not many rooms can accommodate one — least of all, one would think, this 8′ × 11′ area. The canopy, however, is a fanciful fake that makes the most of a sloped ceiling in a small space. The effect is created by attaching lightweight tubular curtain rods to the ceiling, then shirring gathered white eyelet fabric and a ruffled valance onto the rods.

Photo: Norman Nishimura/Design: Patricia A. Lazor

Photo: Ralph Bogertine

Photo: Armen Kachataurian/Design: William Walker

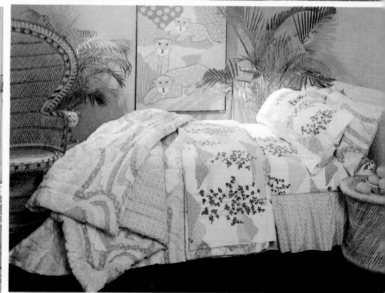

Photo: Pedro E. Guerrerno/Design: Peg White

Photo: Stan Patz

Here are four ways of decorating a room by using coordinating sheets, comforters, and wall coverings.

The French *lit clos* is translated into the Early American idiom. Once-wasted space in the window niche now does double duty as a sitting-sleeping area. Two simple wood frames become headboard and footboard and make the bed fit like a built-in. The frames are padded, then covered with stapled-on check fabric. More check fabric covers bolsters, skirts the bed, and brightens the window wall. A compatible floral print takes over from there, covering the bed and window shades. Matching wallpaper provides a lively background for the warm pine furniture. The tall George Washington chest provides a great deal of storage, and the trestle desk takes readily to dressing table duties.

Design: Virginia Perlo

Here is another version of a *lit clos* — a bed enclosed with fabric. This bed is placed in what used to be a closet, and flowered fabric is run over the walls behind it.

Design: Jim de Martin

➤ Red-and-white gingham, flowers, and washable Dacron fabrics make this holiday-bedecked bedroom a joy all year long. The furniture and carpeting are sophisticated enough to continue being used when the girl has gotten older.

Design: Shirley Regendahl

51

▼ This creamy camel-and-peach bedroom, designed for a teenaged girl, features coordinating furniture and mirrors. Matching fabric covers the walls, bedspread, draperies, and pillows.

▲ What was once a closet is now an out-of-sight vanity-storage area painted shocking pink. Close the folding doors, and the bedroom becomes soft and sweetly old-fashioned, cooled on floor and ceiling by muted green echoes from the traditional print in the wallpaper.

Photos: Vince Lisanti/Design: Nance Randol and Joanne Kinn

Photos: Everette Short/Design: Richard Heizmann

This teenager's suite in a renovated townhouse combines studying and dancing space. The two beds are stored ingeniously off the floor when they are not in use. One raises up to the ceiling via an easy-to-operate counterweight system; the other rolls beneath the raised platform floor of the study area. Two hinged steps and an arch delineate the raised study area. The steps lift so that the trundle bed for sleep-over guests can be stowed beneath the platform. The walls of the upper level are plywood paneling.

Design: Louisa Cowan, ASID

This "candy-box" room has a desk topped by a window-framing "doll house," complete with chimney. Underfoot, brick-patterned nylon carpeting is soft to sit on and keeps spills on top, where they can be sponged up easily. The polka-dot wallpaper conceals finger marks. A strip of wallpaper running around the ceiling outlines acoustical tile in a planked wood pattern. More of the same wallpaper strips form a "ribbon and bow" design on the door. Multi-colored, store-bought storage boxes, which fit into four of the modular units, hold pillows and comforters. Tissue-paper leaves and flowers fill the wall-hung lavabo and blossom on the pegboard lollipop tree.

T he "candy-box" child's room has been re-
done to suit a teenager. Now the beds
are arranged trundle-style. One frame is
upended on top of the other to provide
the sides; the extra mattress slides under the
bed, ready to pull out for sleep-over guests. The
"doll house" was removed to leave the wide desk
top unencumbered. To make it appear larger, the
window is flanked with shutters and covered
with ribbon-trimmed Roman shades. The child-
like cutouts in the chair frames were replaced
with laminated cane table mats. Restacked but
otherwise unchanged, the modular units turn into
end tables for the bedside lamps. The multi-
colored storage boxes were painted white and
striped with the plaid wallpaper. The tall pegboard "lollipop," stripped of its leaves and flowers, now holds a clock.

Photo: Bill Hedrich/Design: Patricia Laughman and J. Christopher Jones

In this girl's room, the bamboo motif of the furniture was incorporated into the custom-designed storage units that form a cushioned banquette. Lattice strips above shirred fabric-covered walls create a gazebo effect in the sleeping/seating area, visually separating it from the study/dressing area. Large- and small-scale print fabrics create an "Alice In Wonderland" effect, enhanced by fluffy clouds billowing overhead in a photomural-covered ceiling.

Design: Ann Heller, ASID

Photo: Photographic Concepts/Design: Patricia Hart McMillan

If you can't have a canopy, consider the luxurious look of a *lit clos*. In this French-accented bedroom, a bed-sized niche is surrounded with fabric. On the bed is an all-cotton, ready-made bedspread topped with pillows sporting shams of the same calico print. Curtains tied back at the sides frame an inviting enclosure. The room's blue color scheme continues underfoot, where a blue-painted floor is stenciled by hand with small white flowers.

Originally, there were no closets in this small bedroom. Since the radiator stuck out anyway, it could be flanked with built-outs that look like built-ins behind their louvered doors. Book-deep introverted shelves maximize storage space at the dressing table "found" when the radiator was boxed in with grillwork panels. A scattering of flowers on the wall covering provides the color cue for the merry window shades.

Photo: Hans Van Nes/Design: Carleton Varney and David Varney

Sweet dreams are a certainty in this dainty bed chamber. The old-fashioned, bow-embellished gingham sheeting is underscored by trim lavished on the headboard, pillows, rocker cushion, café curtains, dust ruffle, and table cover. Diagonal stripes of grosgrain ribbon band the quilted comforter.

Photo: Vince Lisanti/Design: Jerry Gonzalez

▲　This teen dream room is a tri-level arrangement featuring a bed that is at a 45-degree angle from the wall. A desk and table flank one side of the bed, a triangular headboard with recessed planter fills a corner. Drawers and open storage run the length of the other wall.

◄　A glamorous alcove is covered with green wallpaper. Start with a spare closet, or build a frame of plywood edged in wide boards. The bed is merely a plywood platform with a six-inch-thick foam mattress.

Chapter 3
Boys' Rooms

Boys' rooms should have well-thought-out furniture arrangements, with plenty of storage areas and space to display toy, stamp, or other collections. The colors and accessories should be picked carefully to reflect the boy's personality and interests.

Here is a room design for those who need lots of storage and convenience in a relatively small space. Modular, multi-functional units stack against only one wall, making the room seem larger. The glass doors in the modular unit protect books and treasured items. Slide-out tables flank the bed for convenient placement of snacks or a book, slide in when not in use. The compact modular unit leaves the wall across from the bed free to display groupings of art and artifacts, highlighted by track lighting.

Here is a sophisticated, Southwestern-style bedroom. Texture and pattern are the important elements, as shown in the decorative window shades, sisal floor covering, hand-woven pillows and tapestry, and authentic Indian blankets. Dried flowers and flourishing green plants are reflected in the mirrored screen.

Photos: Kent Oppenheimer

Photo: Denes Saari/Design: Donal O'Donnell, ASID

Blondie, Andy Capp, Peanuts, and their colorful cohorts paper this boys' room wall. To convert your favorite funny-paper characters into a wall covering, put them up with wheat paste. A life-size soft sculpture reclines on the lower bunk, a ski boot bank adorns the oak desk, and a cigar store Indian tops the chest.

Photo: Everette Short/Design Evan Frances, ASID, and J. Christopher Jones

The bedspread, bolsters, and shades provide the pattern in this room. Two walls are accented with red-orange paint — the rest are white. A portable television and a phone sit on the desk/dresser combination.

Photo: Vince Lisanti/Design: Gordon Cremers

One wall in this room is covered with wallpaper, the others with a combination of fabrics. The earth-tone color scheme is carried throughout with warm wood furniture and woven wood blinds.

Photos: Randolph Graff/Design: Patricia Cartell

This dream-come-true child's room has a double-decker, "sleep box" bed and lots of colorful storage units. Plastic bins bearing books and toys are wheeled wherever there's space for them. More toys take over the upper level of the sleep box, which also offers an auxiliary play or sleeping area. It's the pizazz of primary colors that gives the room its personality. Ceiling, doors, and moldings are orange, walls gold. The orange bean-bag chair conforms to anyone's shape, and the yellow-painted antique desk is suitable for small people only. On the walls are appealing decals.

Photo: Kent Oppenheimer

Any youngster would be happily at home in this Indian bedroom. To reach the elevated bed alcove, formed by placing a mattress on the built-in storage cabinets, the active young occupant can choose to climb carpeted steps on either side. Sand-colored walls set off accents in appropriately Indian tones of red, navy, and gold; the red thunderbird in the bed recess stretches its massive wings to encompass the adjoining walls. And to complete the color scheme, the sand-colored carpeting bears a border in the same smashing red, navy, and gold.

Photo: Bill Hedrick/Design: Patricia Laughman and J. Christopher Jones

Slipcovered foam pads in coordinating fabrics nestle under a loft for overnight buddies in this boys' bedroom. A third harmonious pattern is introduced in the carpeting. These patterns are played off a light wall color and three light wood finishes, which provide maximum visual and physical space for two active brothers. The loft crosses the large window at the end of the room without blocking the natural light for the areas above and below. Light control is provided for the sleeping area by the use of a thin slat venetian blind. Two night stands are topped by a piece of painted wood to provide a desk, and storage cubes slide neatly under the table that serves as end tables for both beds.

Many interior designers contend that the most successful color scheme is white plus a bold color. Here, it is red and white. "Sylvester" the cat was applied to the wall with washable wall paint. The horizontal bars of the graphic match the color-coordinated, custom-designed mini-blinds.

Photo: Vince Lisanti/Design: Gordon Cremers

65

◄ Wave the flag in a boy's room window with
a Roman shade in Old Glory colors.

Boys can be boys in this imaginative, multi-
purpose bedroom. Even going to bed is fun
when twin beds stack above one another at right
angles. The double desk has overhead lighting
for study and separates the sleeping quarters
from the play area.

Photos: Vince Lisanti/Design: Jerry Gonzalez

This view of the boys' bedroom includes
dressers and floor-to-ceiling shelves that, like the
beds, expand the room size by utilizing air space
rather than floor space. Cantilevered shelves
break the symmetry and permit showcasing of
favorite things. Covered in durable plastic lami-
nate, these brightly colored units can take plenty
of roughhousing.

Growing up can be fun for two boys, who can share this room without getting in each other's way. The reason: A well-designed furniture arrangement. Bunk beds, topped with striking picture blowups, are placed to take the least amount of room. Each boy has his share of dresser drawers, cabinets, and shelves, and his own clothes closet. While one studies at the desk, the other can do so on the bunk bed, which is lighted by a wall-hung fixture. Track lights over the laurel-oak-paneled wall supplement the desk lamp and swivel to heighten general illumination. Curved rattan chairs and an ottoman (more storage in this piece) accommodate the boys' friends. Fabric in an American Indian theme makes tidy coverlets for the bed and sheathes a lambrequin that frames louver vertical blinds. Deep-blue carpeting cues the color of the bedside wall. Plaster sculpture blue jeans are paired with a clock to decorate the wall.

Photos: Floyd Jillson / Design: June Gussin

A modular storage unit with adjacent pier cabinet, mirror, shelves, and drawers provides ample storage for a child's musts and whims. The bed is a combination trundle and bunk — the trundle sleeps an overnight guest and slides out for easy bed-making. The drop-lid desk is attached to the bed, forming the bed's footboard and providing a neat place for study. Beneath the window, with its equestrian stained-glass panel, sits a sea chest. Red accents spice the neutral color scheme.

▼   A bedroom that almost stands up and sa-lutes suits two patriotic young people. No parti-san politics prevail here: George Washington's is the larger-than-life face that, along with red blinds, punctuates the room-wrapping blue arrow. The "Stars and Stripes" bedspreads and the red, white, and blue accessories complete the look.

Photos: Everette Short/Design: John Mascheroni and J. Christopher Jones

Photo: Eastman Studio/Design: Peg Walker

69

A window canopy thatched with knotted fringe sets a safari theme for a small hunter's habitat. The spears that support it and the box-pleated cafés are really wrought-iron drapery rods, also used to hold up the hanging cushion "headboard" for his cot.

Paneling with a rustic texture and grain and a batik-look fabric bedspread in handsome blues and browns give this room a comfortable look.

Photos: Vince Lisanti/Design: Arthur Burke, ASID

This small room is set up to make the best use of the limited space. There are lots of shelves for storage and display space, and a floor bin provides storage for bulky clothing.

Photo: Keith Scott Morton/Design: Scruggs-Myers & Assoc.

Photo: Yuichi Idaka/Design: Richard Honquest and J. Christopher
   Jones

The dark-oak-paneled walls of this boy's room are an exciting background for primitive motifs. A noteworthy design element is the paneling, which was applied on a diagonal above the chair rail and on the horizontal below the chair rail. A high shelf around two walls of the room holds toys, books, and plants. A large woven rug with Mexican motif hangs to the left of the headboard, and a small red rug accents the area over the desk. The fabric for the bedspread and Roman shade hung with a brass rod is a patchwork geometric that picks up the blues, browns, and reds found elsewhere in the house.

71

Chapter 4
Babies' Rooms

A well-designed nursery should get maximal use of its space while needing minimal maintenance. It should be a stimulating place — with bright walls and colorful mobiles. And, if planned right, you should still be able to use its basic furnishings when your child has outgrown the nursery.

This quilt, with patches of children's artwork, makes a beautiful wall hanging.

Photo: Dubbel's Country Studio

*Photos: Harr, Hedrich-Blessing/Design: Claire Golan, ASID, Assoc.
and Mark Golan*

This beautiful baby's room has no-wax, cushioned vinyl flooring. A machine-washable bathroom carpet, thrown over the vinyl flooring, is perfect for romping with the baby. The curtains and window shade are made from dress fabric. Two-tone walls carry out the sunny color scheme.

This unisex environment can be created before the birth of the baby. It was designed to look like the outside of a country cottage. Outdoorsy effects are all over, starting with washable simulated-shingle wall covering and grass-green indoor/outdoor floor covering. Beneath A-shaped yellow cornices resembling roof lines, light filters through yellow blinds spiked with stripes of green. Hand-painted flora fills the room — including scattered wildflowers, a tree inside the door, and giant sunflowers surrounding the crib.

▲   Replace the crib with a bed and the room design can still be used when the baby gets older.

◄   The colors of the walls, banquette, and pillows in this cheerful baby's room were chosen to match those in the wallpaper, and to give the room an outdoorsy effect.

Photo: Darwin Davidson/Design: Jill Wood

Photo: Darwin Davidson/Design: Nina Lee

78

Chapter 5
Guest Rooms

You do not necessarily need a spare bedroom to have a comfortable place for overnight guests. A guest room can be created anywhere you have the space to put a mattress or a sofa bed — in an attic, a den, a living room, or even a dining room.

This guest bedroom gets the down-to-the-last-detail treatment — from the dormer ceiling to the picture frame trim. The usual temptation in decorating a dormer is to stop the wall treatment at the end of the vertical surface; instead, the room here is visually enlarged and heightened by creating a "new ceiling line" through the addition of a simple "bed molding" applied at the horizontal break line. Striped wallpaper runs beyond its vertical wall surface up the dormer wall to meet the molding. Orange and yellow flat braid and loop fringe add punch to the window shades, the bedspread of the high-riser bed, the toss pillows — and even serve as drapery tie-backs. Dress trim and velvet ribbon glamorize a picture frame.

➤ Bold colors highlight this tiny townhouse guest room. The striped shades are vinyl coated, and an extra bit of the shade cloth is used to mask the ugly face of the air conditioner. The spread on the storage bed is a red terry auto seat cover, available from auto parts stores.

This guest room can double as a library or den, for it contains a surprising amount of storage space and includes a desk. The simple lines of the 18-inch-deep modular furniture pieces are reminiscent of·Shaker design. The queen-sized bed does not appear to crowd the room because it "floats" on a platform. Note the special effect of the polished aluminum track lighting, which highlights a "brick" wall, the color and texture of which lend drama to the other neutral walls of the room. An airy print in beige and apricot makes a charming coverlet that coordinates without matching the geometric pattern in the louvered blind. Light-hearted accessories include the coy Japanese ladies framed in half rounds above the bed and a wall hanging of Indian dancers. A whimsical "spook" light on the night stand beside the bed and two Oriental- inspired lamps lend coziness as well as light for reading and writing.

Photo: Floyd Jillson/Design: June Gussin

Photo: Richard Champion/Design: Carleton Varney

Lavished all over the bedroom, crispy gingham is always refreshing. Bright lemon yellow
accents the ceiling and table.

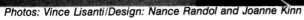

Photos: Vince Lisanti/Design: Nance Randol and Joanne Kinn

◄ This blue and beige guest room can double as a study. The handsome oak-finished furniture offers a place for everything — typewriter, television, stereo, and tape deck. The closet holds a comforter and linens.

Washable vinyl wall covering adorns the walls and the window shade of this gray, pumpkin, and beige Art Deco bedroom. A wall recliner provides comfortable seating without taking up too much space. The bed's headboard is a plywood arc covered with gray polished cotton and shirred around the edge.

Photo: Photographic House/Design: Margot Gunther, ASID

▲   The velveteen bower is bound to be the softest bedroom on the block. It only *looks* like an extravagance, with printed cotton velveteen wrapping the walls like a comfortable cocoon. You can do it all yourself, even the elegantly gathered headboard that so richly mates the quilted bedspread. To cover your walls with fabric, you'll need a staple gun and enough velveteen to allow at least double fullness.

➤   Here's a cushy stack of round bolsters, cut in half and covered with sheets to match the dust ruffle and draperies.

◄ An English chintz-look floral with a dark background creates an intimate feeling in this attic bedroom. Doors and trim are antiqued to blend softly with the paper. Solid-color fabrics in luxurious textures for the bed and dressing area emphasize the elegance reflected by the paper. The elaborate brass fireplace fan and a gold leaf mirror in the adjoining dressing area carry out the opulent look.

Photos: Alderman Studio/Design: Patricia Plaxico, ASID

▲ Here is another way to decorate the same attic room. A vigorous red-and-green chintz pattern covers the walls and ceiling, bed, footstool, cushions, mirror frame, and dressing table! It just proves there's no such thing as too much of a good thing when the pattern is this pretty. (A word of caution — a large-scaled pattern might not be so easy to live with.) An off-white paint for the doors and trim matches the paper's background and maintains the sunny mood of the sprightly pattern.

Photo: Photographic House/Design: Patricia Hart McMillan

With a good book, a rocking chair, and a cup of tea, your guest can have a quiet morning in this haven. The cheery room offers easy maintenance and plenty of privacy.

Photo: Ernest Silva/Design: Margot Gunther

Space savvy turned a tiny bedroom into a chic contemporary creation. A geometric print patterns walls and window shade, tailors the platform bed and pillow shams; the print continues on screens that form a dramatic dimensional headboard, which can conceal a desk or storage area. A touch of "high tech": Industrial clay pipes with a slab of slate form a unique table.

Photo: Hans Van Nes/Design: Shirley Regendahl

The bright-blue painted floor and walls are a background echo of the enchanting fabric on the ceiling, built-in window seat, closet doors, draperies, shades, and bedspread.

A touch of pink in this guest bedroom adds an extra dimension to the yellow-and-green color scheme. The wall covering spreads a field of flowers around the bedroom and into the adjoining bath.

Photo: Darwin Davidson/Design: Evan Frances, ASID, and Sally Alcorn

87

Photo: Hedrich-Blessing/Design: Montgomery Ward Home Furnishings Staff

Photo: Ernest Silva/Design: Margot Gunther

A queen-sized guest bed stows in a pull-out drawer beneath the platform in the living room. The sofa, usually pushed against the platform, is moved a few feet to the entrance area when the bed is in use.

Dressed in seersucker, gingham, ruffles, and bows, this old-fashioned bedroom wears a home-sewn wardrobe in pretty patterns, coordinated in fabric and wall covering. The double-skirted table is a convenient spot for sipping coffee.

◄ This room was converted from a child's room to a guest room by covering the walls with vinyl wallpaper, which is coordinated with the solid green, linen-textured fabric on the screen, bench, and lambrequin. The small-checked cotton gingham spread and cushions add to the restful mood.

▼ This sophisticated mother-in-law retreat was designed to be multi-functional. It's a setting for quiet, special moments: letter-writing, an intimate dinner, or an elegant snack. The colorful patchwork fabric sets the scheme — a mélange of reds with a dollop of emerald green as an accent. The nostalgic-look mirror has been hung close to the fireplace mantel, giving it the appearance of an architectural detail. The true architectural details — the doors, mantelpiece, trim, and moldings — are painted semi-gloss cream. The ceiling has been left white to reflect soft light from the lamps. Up-lights under the plants add to the subtle lighting effects. For safety's sake, area rugs are secured to the floor with a mastic.

Photo: Bob Braun/Design: Warren Arnett

This den-guest room was created from a once dull, dark, and depressing attic. The transformation begins with dark-grained paneling that highlights the architectural excitement of sharply angled dormers. The dormer and wall paneling was applied horizontally. Ceiling paneling was applied perpendicularly to make the room look larger and avoid a closed-in-a-box feeling. A cluster of three smoked-glass light fixtures illuminates the dramatic stairwell with a soaring wall pierced by windows stacked at two levels. Like all the guest-room windows, these have black blinds that emphasize the dark grain of the paneling and control the light while inviting the view. To warm and unify the space and add texture to its smooth wood and glass surfaces, a nylon carpet swathes the floor. The carpeting also muffles noise so occupants of the master bedroom below can snooze even while there's reveling above. A pair of brass beds have bolsters and cushions to make them comfortable by day.

Photo: Alan Hicks/Design: Russ English and Mark Perry

Here are two different ways of covering bedroom windows. (Top) Crisp white shutters with adjustable louvers control light and provide needed privacy. (Bottom) The shade is laminated with lightweight fabric. (Heavy fabric won't roll; too light won't hang well.) A plywood lambrequin frames the window.

Design: Marjorie Scholly, ASID

Design: John Hayden, ASID

▲   The guest suite shown here is furnished for a mother-in-law in full-time residence and is a self-contained private hideaway. Designed for personal comfort and small-scale entertaining, it has a large living area, dining corner, private bath, and roomy walk-in closet. The sleep sofa opens to a queen-sized bed. And the double-skirted round table has a glass top for quick and easy cleanup. A lifetime of mementos are prominently displayed in a large, open-shelved, turn-o-the-century parlor cabinet with dressing mirror and storage space. The folding screen has shirred panels of sheer lacy fabric. Thoughtful amenties include a telephone, radio, television, and (not in picture) ceiling fan with light to provide gentle air movement and overhead lighting.

Photo: Keith Scott Morton/Design: Alan Scruggs

Fresh flowers in a spatterware pot accent a floral-bedecked bedroom. The window-seat "sofa" is made by stapling shirred fabric to a plywood base, adding a fabric-covered foam pad and a pile of pillows. Note: A lambrequin in matching wall covering is inside the window frame. Old-fashioned tins, cork-top jars, and books grace a blue-painted baker's rack.

Photo: Vince Lisanti/Design: Nance Randol Interiors

Twin beds swathed with flower-sprigged coverlets share an airy wicker headboard. The old wicker rocker and planter were freshened with spray paint. A wallpaper border runs horizontally just below the ceiling, making the ceiling appear higher.

With a pattern that matches the bedspread, a headboard was created by stretching and stapling fabric onto a plywood frame and securing it to the wall with nails.

A traditional canopy bed becomes crisply contemporary dressed in black and white, and lined in emerald green to brighten the inside view.

Coordinated comforters, pillow shams, and draperies liven up this guest room. The striped comforters reverse to solid blue. The matching draperies and café curtains are pinch-pleated.

Photo: Alderman Studio/Design: Randy Trull, ASID